KT-558-448

Kent
County
Council

owning a pet
DOG

Selina Wood

W
FRANKLIN WATTS
LONDON • SYDNEY

First published in 2005 by
Franklin Watts
96 Leonard Street
London
EC2A 4XD

Franklin Watts Australia
45–51 Huntley Street
Alexandria, NSW 2015

Series editor: Adrian Cole
Series design: Sarah Borny
Art director: Jonathan Hair
Picture researcher: Kathy Lockley
Special photography: Ray Moller
Illustrations by: Hannah Matthews

A CIP catalogue record for this book is
available from the British Library.

ISBN: 0 7496 5925 4

Printed in Malaysia

The author and publisher would like to thank the following people
for their contribution to the production of this book:

Jo, Graham and Toby; Nat Redfern; Jon Spavin and the Alpha Dog Training School

Acknowledgements:
BIOS/Still Pictures: 12 bl
Comstock Images/Alamy: 12 t
© Robert Dowling/CORBIS: 4 t
Dynamic Graphics Group/Creatas/Alamy: 29
Jeff Greenberg/Alamy: 8 cr
Angela Hampton/RSPCA Photolibrary: Cover, 9 t, 12 -13, 28 t
©Andrew Hawkins/CORBIS: 4 b
Juniors Bildarchiv/Alamy: 9 br
The Kennel Club Picture Library 25 b
T.Kitchin & V.Hurst/NHPA: 6 t
Klein/Still Pictures: 5, 17 bl
Yves Lanceau/NHPA: 8 bl
Michael Leach/NHPA: 20 c
Ray Moller 10, 14 b, 17 br, 17 t, 18 c, 23 b, 23 t
PhotoStockFile/Alamy: 22 b
Rex Features 6 b, 7
Alan Robinson/RSPCA Photolibrary: 11
Andy Rouse/NHPA: 21
Jon Spavin 29 c, /Alpha Dog Training School 24 b
TNT MAGAZINE/Alamy 15 t
Dave Watts/NHPA: 20 bl
WTPix 27 b

Contents

Dogs as pets

It is often said that dogs are our best friends. Their high intelligence and loyal, sociable natures make them great companions. Owning a dog is fun and rewarding, but it is a huge commitment too.

Dogs have been popular pets since ancient times. Breeds today vary from small Jack Russells to huge Great Danes and from cuddly toy dogs to energetic hounds. Some dogs make useful workers, while others are just good friends. With more than 400 breeds in the world to choose from, there is a dog to suit almost everyone!

Dogs are energetic and make great companions.

What a dog needs

Dogs rely on humans to meet all their basic needs, such as food, shelter, health, affection and exercise. Before you get a dog or puppy you need to be sure that you can provide all these things, every day, for the whole of the animal's life. Puppies grow up quickly, and most dogs live for at least 12 years. Think ahead and decide if you're ready for this long-term responsibility.

DUTY OF CARE

RSPCA International has outlined five basic rights that should be granted to all pets:

- **Freedom from hunger and thirst**
- **Freedom from discomfort**
- **Freedom from pain, injury and disease**
- **Freedom to express normal behaviour**
- **Freedom from fear and distress**

"Looking after Monty can be hard work at times, but he's worth it!"

A well-kept dog will form a strong bond with its owner. If you care for your dog, it will love you in return.

ASK YOURSELF

- Do you have the time to care for a dog properly? If you're not around, you'll need to find someone else to look after it.
- Do you and your family have enough money to keep a dog happy and healthy? Dog food and vet bills are expensive.
- Do you have space for a dog to live comfortably, and somewhere to walk it every day? Dogs like to explore and exercise.

A strong relationship

If you can offer a dog a good home, make the most of the opportunity. A dog can teach you a lot, as well as be a great playmate. It will love you, look up to you and even protect you. But you should always remember that dogs are very different from human beings. It's easy to assume that a dog is somehow a younger version of you, but it has very different instincts, which you should always respect.

Dogs and people

Dogs have been valued by humans for many thousands of years, but their ancestors have lived in the wild for much longer. Pet dogs are descended from wolves. They all belong to the *Canidae* (dog) family.

The first domestic dogs

Wolves were first tamed, or domesticated, over 12,000 years ago. Experts think this happened as wolves scavenged around human settlements, and people started to use them as guards and hunting assistants. Dogs' sociable and co-operative natures helped them to fit in with human groups.

Humans trained wolves to help them hunt for food.

How breeds developed

Over the centuries, humans bred dogs for certain tasks. Two dogs that were good at herding livestock, for instance, were bred together to produce an even better herder. Gradually, different breeds were developed. For example, dogs in Arctic regions were bred to pull sledges, and large, fierce dogs were even trained to fight in battles.

Today, dogs don't fight in battles. But they are used to guard military sites.

This German Shepherd is using its sense of smell to locate people trapped after an earthquake and landslip.

Working dogs

Today, most dogs are brought up as family pets. Some are bred to compete in dog shows. But others are still working animals. The dog's keen sense of smell, for instance, helps police uncover drugs and bombs, and even to find victims of earthquakes. Dogs are experts at leading the blind and deaf, and many provide physical support for disabled people. Some are even used in therapy, to help people with emotional problems or comfort families who have suffered a tragedy.

THERAPY DOGS

The affection of a friendly dog can be a useful form of therapy. Dogs are now used as rehabilitation aids in nursing homes, childcare centres and even at disaster sites. Following the terrorist attacks on 11 September 2001, dogs were brought into Red Cross centres to help relieve the distress for rescuers and families who had lost loved-ones in the attacks. Dogs are also used by some physical therapists to help improve patients' co-ordination and fitness through games and other exercises.

Which breed?

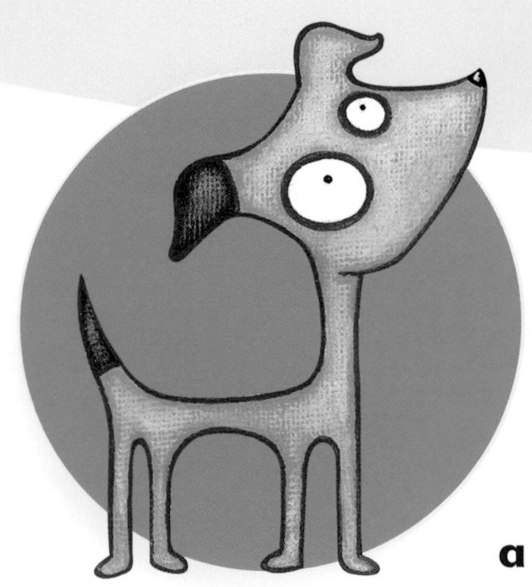

Knowing about dog breeds will help you when you choose a pet dog. Purebred dogs are bred over many generations to look alike. Mixed-breed dogs are a combination of different breeds.

TERRIERS

Terriers are small, tough and lively – they were originally bred for hunting rats and mice. Their lively personalities make them appealing as pets, though they can sometimes be aggressive.

Examples: Border Terrier, Jack Russell, Yorkshire Terrier, West Highland White Terrier

TOY DOGS

Toy dogs are small dogs bred to be people's companions. They have strong characters and are often noisy, but they don't need as much exercise as the bigger breeds.

Examples: Bichon Frise, Chihuahua (above), Pekingese, Pug

HOUNDS

Hounds were bred to chase and hunt animals. These medium-to-large dogs are usually very friendly, but they need a lot of exercise.

Examples: Greyhound, Afghan Hound, Beagle (left)

WORKING DOGS

Working dogs are traditional guard and rescue dogs. Although loyal and intelligent, they do not make ideal first pets as they are often large and strong, and can be over-protective.

Examples: Boxer, Doberman, Great Dane, St Bernard

PASTORAL (HERDING) DOGS

Pastoral dogs are best known for herding sheep and cattle. They are intelligent, easy to train and have lots of energy. As pets they may get bored and restless if they don't have enough to do.

Examples: Collie, German Shepherd (left), Old English Sheepdog, Samoyed

GUN DOGS

Gun dogs were originally bred to help hunters retrieve shot-down game. Many of them are co-operative and make great family pets, as long as they get plenty of exercise.

Examples: Cocker Spaniel, Irish Setter, Labrador Retriever

UTILITY DOGS

Utility dogs have been bred over the years for different purposes. They include a wide variety of breeds that don't fit into any of the other groups.

Examples: Bulldog, Chow-chow, Dalmatian, Poodle

Dalmatians, like this puppy, are one of the most popular utility breeds.

MIXED BREEDS

Mixed-breed dogs (or mongrels) are mixtures of two or more breeds. They tend to be healthier than purebreds; they are also cheaper to buy and generally make good pets. However, it is often difficult to predict their final size and temperament.

Rescue centres often have many mixed-breed dogs to choose from.

Choosing a dog

When you're thinking of buying a dog, it's important to choose one that suits your lifestyle. Take into account its adult size, temperament and daily needs. Find out as much as you can about a dog before you buy it.

A large dog won't be happy in a small house. A noisy dog may disturb a quiet neighbourhood. If you hate going for long walks, an energetic dog is not for you. Think about the way your family works, and bear in mind other pets or young children in your home – some dogs are more tolerant than others.

SOME POPULAR BREEDS COMPARED

	Size	Nature	Exercise needs	Trainability
Beagle	Medium	Friendly	High	Low/average
Bichon Frise	Small	Playful	Low	High
Border Terrier	Small	Vivacious	Moderate	Average/high
Cocker Spaniel	Medium	Cheerful	Moderate	Average/high
Collie	Medium	Willing	High	High
Golden Retriever	Large	Enthusiastic	High	High
Labrador Retriever	Large	Devoted	High	High
Pekingese	Small	Independent	Low	Low/average
Pug	Small	Show-off	Low	Average
Whippet	Medium	Sensitive	Moderate	Average

PICKING A PUP

What to look for in a new puppy:

- **alertness**
- **friendliness**
- **calm nature**
- **fluffy fur with no sore patches**
- **a plump (but not fat) body**
- **a clean rear**
- **bright eyes**
- **a cool, damp nose**

Puppies are very cute, but they need round-the-clock care and attention until they become more confident.

Prepared for a pup?

A puppy needs someone to be around all the time while it settles in. It may chew things and have accidents while it is toilet training. But it will be a great playmate and will bond with you quickly. Make sure you're prepared for its needs as an adult, too. It's relatively easy to predict how a purebred puppy will turn out. If you're buying a mixed breed, try to find out the size and temperament of both its parents.

BUYING A DOG

Look for a breeder or rescue centre that really cares about their dogs' futures. Ask your vet about the best places to go – avoid puppy farms, dealers or pet shops. Try to visit the dog in its home environment, with its mother and siblings. Staff at rescue centres can help you choose a suitable dog. They will want to inspect your home, to make sure the dog will be happy and well cared for.

Buying an adult

If you don't have time to care for and train a puppy, consider getting an adult dog. It should be easier to look after, but check its health and history.

Settling in

When you first take your dog home it will feel anxious, especially if it has come straight from a litter. Introduce it to people gradually and create an environment that will make it feel at home.

A comfy bed

A dog needs one area of the house that it can regard as its own territory. Buy a basket and fill it with soft, washable bedding. Put it in a quiet corner. If you're bringing home a young puppy, consider a puppy crate. This is like a pen where the puppy can eat and sleep while it gets used to its new surroundings.

A basket and blanket absorb your dog's scent, so it feels safe. Use baskets and bedding made of materials that can't be easily chewed and swallowed.

Keeping tabs

Buy your dog a lead and an identity collar that fits well. You should be able to get two fingers between the collar and your dog's neck – keep checking this as your puppy grows. It may try to scratch the collar off at first, but will soon get used to it. For extra security, you could get a micro identity chip injected painlessly by a vet.

Buy your dog an identity collar. If your dog ever gets lost, a collar will help to identify it.

"Make sure your dog's bed is in a safe place that it has access to throughout the day."

Pet peace

Many dogs can be taught to get along with other pets, even cats, if they socialise at an early age. But you should always try to watch them when they are together. If you already have another dog, make sure it accepts the new arrival and doesn't get into fights.

Travelling

If you travel in a car, it's a good idea to get your dog used to it. Take it with you on short journeys at first, in case it is travel sick. You should never leave a dog in a car, even in cool weather. It could get heatstroke and die. Every year dogs die in cars – don't let yours.

HOUSE DOS AND DON'TS

Dogs love to explore and chew things, so make sure your house is a hazard-free zone.

DO put away anything that may be harmful to your dog, such as poisonous cleaning fluids and house plants, sharp knives, and small objects that can be swallowed.

DO unplug electrical equipment. Chewing the wires could give your dog a deadly electric shock.

DO put up child gates if there are parts of the house you want to be dog-free.

DO have some old newspapers to hand for toilet training.

DON'T leave a small puppy alone in the house.

DON'T leave rubbish lying around in bags or in bins that can be knocked over.

DON'T leave food uncovered on surfaces that your dog can reach.

DON'T leave outside doors, low windows or garden gates open. Make sure there are no gaps in the garden hedge or fence.

DON'T leave a dog loose with other pets.

Feeding time

As your dog settles in, establish a routine for feeding. Pet dogs are not like their wild relatives, who are usually pure carnivores, they need a balanced diet. Find out from your vet what your dog needs.

Regular meals

It's important that you set regular mealtimes for your dog, and don't suddenly change its diet. Try to feed it at the same time each day and avoid giving it too many snacks or treats in between. A puppy will eat little and often, while an adult dog requires fewer, larger meals. Make the changes gradually as your dog grows up.

Age	Meals per day
8–12 weeks	4
13–16 weeks	3
6 months	2
10 months	2 small (*small breeds*) 1 main + 1 small (*large breeds*)
adult	2 small (*small breeds*) 1 main (*large breeds*)

Dog food

There are three main types of dog food. Complete canned food and complete dried food are easy to store and contain all the nutrients a dog needs. If your dog prefers tinned or fresh meat, you should mix it with dog biscuits to give a balanced diet. Puppy food is different from dog food – check with your vet that you're buying the right type.

Use a sturdy bowl for feeding your dog, and wash it out well after each meal.

"Your dog should be eager to eat, but not pushy – don't let it jump up while you're preparing its food."

Water

Like all pets, dogs need constant access to fresh drinking water. Put a bowl in a safe corner on the floor, and wash and refill it every day.

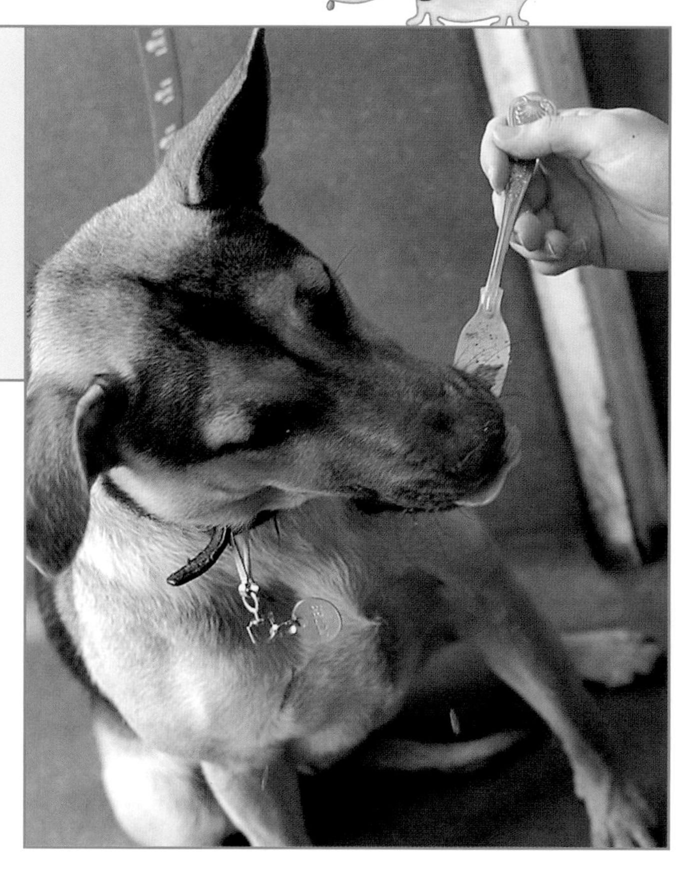

Never feed your dog like this. Forks or other utensils could damage it's mouth. Use a bowl or your fingers.

Weight watchers

A dog that is fed too much will become overweight, and this can shorten its lifespan. Make sure your dog gets the right amount to eat. It should be sleek and fit – if you can't feel its ribs, it is probably too fat. If its ribs poke out, it may be too thin. Check with your vet.

Worming

One cause of weight loss could be worms. To prevent them, your dog will need worming every 3 to 6 months. Ask your vet for the correct dosage. It will usually come as a powder or tablet that you can slip into your dog's food.

Medication can often be given to your dog in its food.

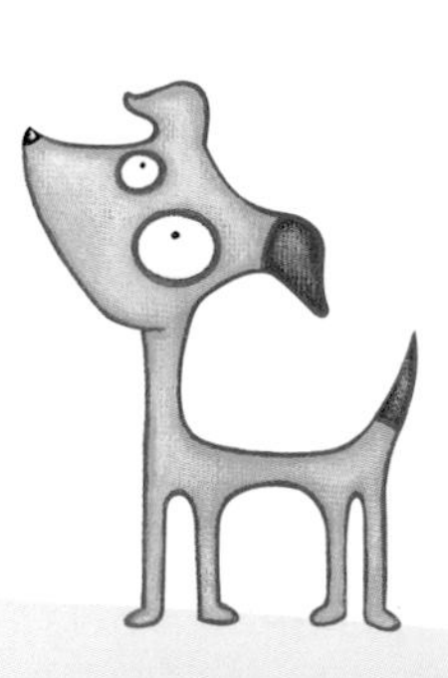

Exercise and play

Like you, dogs need plenty of attention and regular exercise. Otherwise they can become unfit and overweight. Remember that it's cruel to leave your dog for hours on its own.

Going for walks

Set a time for regular walks. The amount of exercise your dog needs will depend on its breed and its age. The most energetic dogs need to walk several kilometres a day and will rarely tire. Even if you have a less active breed, daily exercise is important to keep its joints and heart healthy. A lively run around the house may be enough for some toy breeds, but aim to take your dog out for a walk at least twice a day.

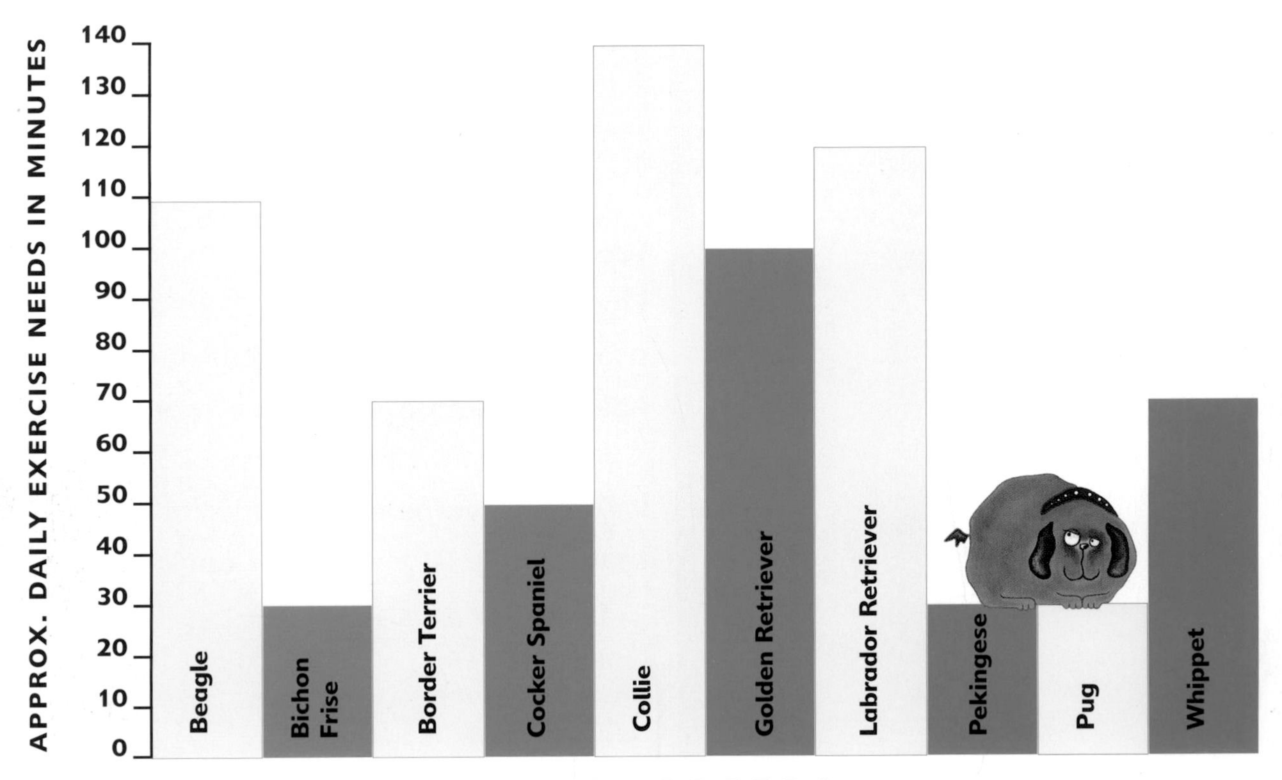

"At first Toby always tried to take me for a walk! So we went to training classes – find out if there's one in your area."

Your dog needs plenty of room to walk in front of you, but should not pull on the lead.

Out and about

When you are out you should always keep your dog under control. Find a place, such as a park, where your dog has plenty of room to play. Only let it off the lead where there are no roads, and when you have trained your dog to come to you (see pages 22–23). Don't let it chase other people or animals.

Puppy play

Young puppies should not be taken for walks, as they can pick up diseases from other animals. You should play with them at home until they have completed a course of vaccinations (see page 21).

Dog toys come in many shapes and sizes and are good for games such as fetch and hide-and-seek.

SHOWING RESPECT

When you're out walking, take a plastic bag or pooper scooper so you can clean up any messes. Be respectful to other people who may not feel as comfortable with dogs as you do. Make sure you know where you can and can't take your dog in your local area.

Grooming and care

Your dog's wellbeing depends on other things as well as food and exercise. You must also maintain its general condition so that it looks and feels healthy.

Grooming

If your dog has a long coat, you'll need to comb and brush it every day to keep it clean and free of tangles. Dogs with short or medium coats should be groomed once or twice a week. Use a dog comb and bristle brush for longer coats, and a rubber slicker for short coats. Some curly-coated dogs, such as Poodles, may need special grooming by an expert.

Grooming your dog will help get rid of loose hairs, and most dogs enjoy being rubbed-down too!

COAT LENGTHS

Long coats	**Medium coats**	**Short coats**
Afghan Hound	Bichon Frise	Beagle
Chow-chow	Border Terrier	Boxer
Collie	Cocker Spaniel	Dalmatian
English Sheepdog	German Shepherd	Labrador Retriever
Pekingese	Golden Retriever	Pug
Shih-tzu	Samoyed	Whippet

"Dogs don't like getting soap in their eyes. Sponge your dog carefully, and never use a human shampoo."

BATHING

A dog doesn't need bathing very often – just once or twice a year, or if it gets covered in dirt. Always use a special dog shampoo and keep a towel spare for drying. Try not to bath puppies younger than six months old – any dry mud on their coat will usually brush out.

Parasites

While you're grooming your dog, check its coat and ears for parasites including fleas, mites and ticks. If your dog is scratching more than usual, use a flea comb and look for small, black specks. Black wax in the ears is a sign of mites, while ticks appear as small cream or grey lumps on the skin. All these bugs are easy to treat. Ask your vet for advice.

CLAW CARE

A dog's claws normally wear down naturally on the ground, but sometimes they may grow too long and become painful. Let a vet show you how to clip your dog's claws correctly.

Healthy teeth

Dental care is important for dogs, too. Cleaning your dog's teeth once a week with a special canine toothpaste and brush should prevent inflamed gums and other problems. Dog toys to chew on can also help to keep teeth and gums healthy.

In the wild

The *Canidae* family includes numerous wild species, including wolves, foxes and dingoes. Unlike pets, these untamed carnivores are highly adaptable and able to take care of themselves.

Pack instinct

Most members of the *Canidae* family hunt in packs. Individuals work together to hunt prey that would normally be too big to tackle on their own. When they've caught the prey, they share the kill. The dominant male gets the biggest share.

Feral dogs

Australia's wild dog, the dingo, is feral – a domesticated species that has become wild again. It was introduced to Australia about 4,000 years ago. Dingoes usually hunt alone, unless they are hunting large prey, such as kangaroos.

Dingoes, like this one, are often shot because they kill sheep.

Foraging foxes

There are 10 species in the fox group. Red foxes are the most common, occurring in many different environments including deserts, mountains and inner city areas. They hunt on their own and eat a range of food, from rodents and insects to scraps from people's rubbish. You might have seen one rifling through dustbins in your street (above).

Family first

Jackals and coyotes are wild dogs that live in close-knit family groups. They hunt together and bring back food for any pups in the den. They patrol their territory and make scent-markers with their urine and faeces to deter any intruders.

Under threat

Wild dogs can be found in a wide range of habitats, from Arctic tundra to scorching deserts. Hunting and habitat destruction, however, have reduced populations, and many species are endangered. Conservation and breeding programmes are attempting to protect these animals and bring them to people's attention.

This African Wild Dog is one of many endangered Canidae.

Endangered *Canidae* include:

- Red Wolf (North America)
- Simian Jackal (Ethiopia)
- Island Grey Fox (Californian Channel Islands)
- African Wild Dog (Central and Southern Africa)
- Bush Dog (Northern South America)
- Maned Wolf (South America)

Dog behaviour

Dogs have a body language all of their own, much of which stems from their ancestors in the wild. If you make an effort to understand it, you'll have a happier relationship with your dog.

Barking

Dogs bark or whine when they want your attention, often because they want to play or go to the toilet. They also bark as a warning – for example, when a stranger comes to the house. An excited dog will bark, too. The various types of bark all sound a bit different.

Tail talk

Tail wagging indicates excitement and friendliness. A tail between the legs is a sign of sadness or submission. An upright tail means alertness and dominance. If your dog chases its tail, it is probably bored.

Growling or howling

Dogs display aggression when they don't want to let go of something, or when they're afraid or in pain. They hold their tails straight and the fur on their neck stands up. If a dog growls you should back off. Howling is a distress call. Dogs howl to let you know where they are or when they are lonely.

Dogs, especially young ones, often fight, tumble and growl at each other. But they are usually just playing.

"I used to hate it when other dogs came up to sniff my dog. But it's just their way of finding out about each other."

Senses

Dogs have acute senses of smell and hearing. They will notice someone approaching your door long before you do, and will prick up their ears with interest. Dogs' eyes are very sensitive to movement, but they don't see colour in the same way as humans do.

Scent signals

Dogs produce scents to communicate with each other. That's why dogs sniff each other when they meet, and mark out territory with urine or faeces.

When a dog finds a strong scent it will often cover it with its own urine.

When it lies on its back to have its tummy stroked, a dog is showing you that it knows you're the boss!

PACK PET

The way your dog responds to people has links with its wolf ancestry. Your dog will think of your family as a pack (see page 20), with a natural leader who may be your parent. A bold, untrained dog may think that he or she is the leader!

Training your dog

Teaching your dog to respond to you will make your life easier and keep your dog happy and safe. You should start training a puppy straight away, so that it doesn't develop too many bad habits.

Toilet training

You'll need to toilet train a puppy when you first bring it home. Take it outside every couple of hours, especially after sleeping, eating and drinking. At first you could let your puppy urinate indoors on newspapers. Move the newspapers nearer to the door each day, and then outside.

Socialising

Young puppies need to be taught how to behave. Introduce them to people and animals slowly so that they're not overwhelmed. They should also learn to be left on their own for a short time, so they don't get distressed every time you leave the room.

Take your dog to a training school where you can learn to train it correctly.

TRAINING TIPS

- Use your dog's name as much as possible while training.
- Be encouraging. Always praise your dog or give it a dog treat when it does something right.
- Be firm but don't lose your temper. NEVER hit your dog. Training is all about patience.
- You can go on special courses to learn to train your dog. Contact the Kennel Club (see page 31).

Commands

Start teaching your dog commands. Teach it to recognise its name and the word 'no'. Always say 'no' in a firm voice and back it up with a body signal, such as waving a finger. Make sure everyone in your family uses the same word and signal for each command.

COME!

To train your dog to come to you, crouch down with your arms open and shout your pet's name and then the word 'come'. When your dog comes, reward it with a dog treat. Gradually increase the distance between you. It's best to keep your dog on a long, retractable lead at first, until you're sure it won't run off.

SIT! STAY!

Teach your dog to sit by raising a dog treat over your head so that the dog has to sit down to see it. At the same time say 'sit' firmly. When your dog sits, praise it and give it the treat. To teach it to stay, put your hand out flat towards the dog's face and say 'stay' slowly. Keep repeating this as you gradually move away. If your dog gets up, try again.

WHAT'S IN A NAME?

Dogs respond best to short names with one or two syllables. Pick something that's easy to call out, but avoid names that sound like standard instructions such as 'sit', 'fetch', or 'stay'.

You might want to train your dog to compete in competitions. Agility classes are fun for both of you.

Visiting the vet

It's your responsibility to notice when your dog is ill, so look out for the signs. Even if your dog is healthy, you should take it to the vet every year for a check-up.

If you're worried about your dog, telephone or visit the vet straight away. The sooner you catch a problem, the quicker it can be sorted out. The vet should be able to tell you what's wrong, and answer any questions you may have about how to look after your dog.

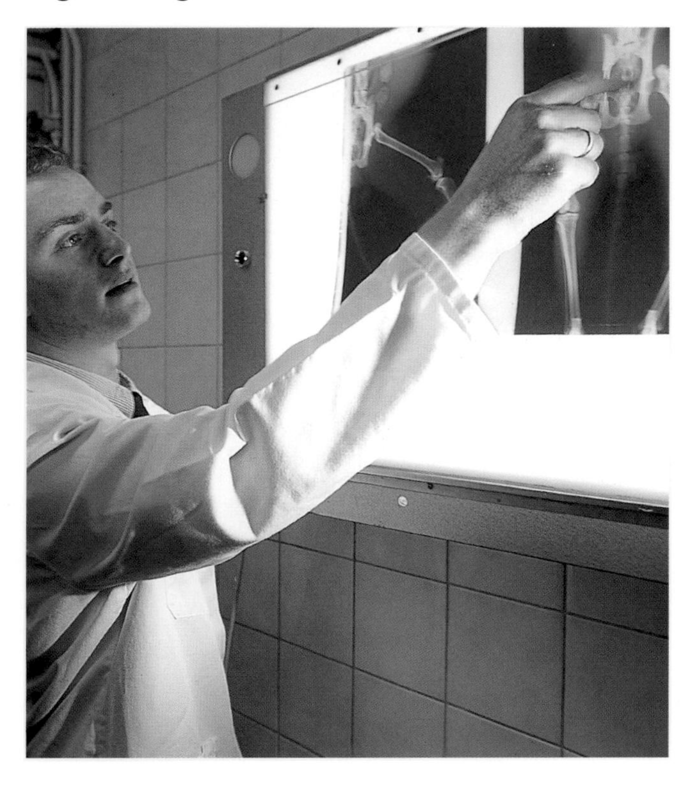

SIGNS YOUR DOG MAY BE ILL

- **Lack of interest in food**
- **Excessive thirst**
- **Diarrhoea (watery faeces)**
- **Shivering**
- **Coughing**
- **Weight loss**
- **Discharge from eyes, nose or ears**
- **Unusually bad temper**
- **Unusually quiet or tired**
- **Any other major changes in behaviour**

"If your dog is involved in an accident, don't panic. Get it to a vet as quickly as possible."

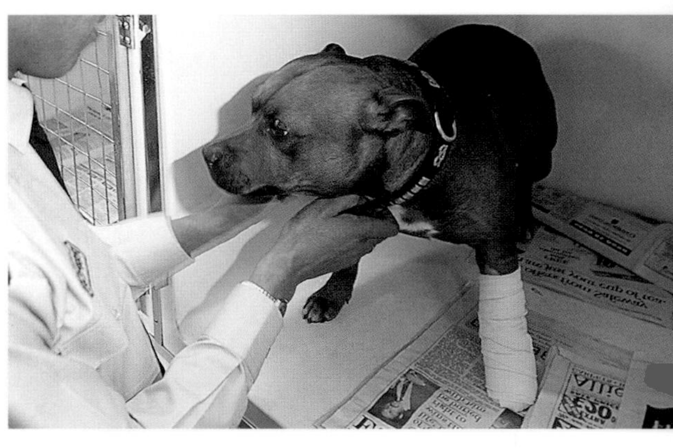
Dogs recover well from most injuries – even broken legs.

Accidents

In the case of a bad accident involving a dog, try to get help from an adult the dog knows. Stop any bleeding by pressing down on the wound with a clean handkerchief. Cover the dog with a blanket to comfort it while you take it to the vet. Carry it in a crate or large box, and avoid moving it too much in case any of its bones are broken.

Jabs and check-ups

Puppies need a series of vaccinations to stop them from getting dangerous dog diseases. The first are given at about eight weeks old. Adult dogs require annual booster jabs. These can be given when you take your dog for its yearly check-up.

Neutering and spaying?

Dogs mature quickly. Before your dog is six months old, you should decide whether you want to have it altered (neutered or spayed). It is a simple operation that stops your dog being able to have puppies. Don't forget, irresponsible breeding is cruel.

These puppies are just a few hours old – their eyes are still shut.

REMEMBER

Think carefully if you decide against altering:

- **Breeding can be very expensive.**
- **A dog (bitch) may have up to 14 puppies in a litter – you'll need to care for them until they're at least seven weeks old.**
- **You will have to find good homes for all of the puppies.**

Losing a pet

Unfortunately, your dog won't live as long as you do. If you look after it well, you will have many happy years together. But accidents do happen and one day even the best-kept dog will die.

Old age

Dogs have much shorter lifespans than we do. They are fully grown within a year, and old by their teens. An old dog may slow down and need to see a vet more often. It may suffer from stiff joints and deafness. It will be sad when your dog dies, so take time to grieve.

DOG YEARS

How old is your dog in human years?
One year = 16 human years
Two years = 24 human years
Three years = 30 human years
Each year after, add five human years.

IF YOUR DOG RUNS AWAY

Your home should be a dog-secure place, with no gaps in the garden fence, and doors and gates kept shut. When you're out walking you should keep your dog on the lead unless you're sure it's a safe area. But dogs can be curious, clever and quick enough to slip away. If yours does escape, act quickly.

- **Go outside and call your dog's name. Try blowing a whistle or squeaking a favourite toy.**
- **Ask friends in the neighbourhood if they've seen your dog.**
- **Check places where your dog likes to go. Perhaps there's another dog in the area that it is friends with.**
- **If all else fails, contact your local vet and rescue centre.**

"Whatever happens in the future, Bonny will always be my best friend."

Accidents and illness

In the case of a serious accident or illness, your vet may suggest putting your dog to sleep. This will only happen if nothing can be done to save it. It is hard to agree to say goodbye for the last time. But it would be unfair to keep your dog alive if it is only going to suffer more.

Losing your dog is hard. Talk about your feelings with family and friends.

Looking back at photographs can be a good way to remember better times spent with your dog.

Happy memories

You will probably feel a whole range of emotions when your dog dies, from anger to guilt. Losing a loyal friend might make you feel lonely or scared. This is normal, but with time you will find ways to fill the gap. Try to think about all the fun you've had together. Whatever you do, don't rush out and buy another dog or puppy straight away or blame yourself for the death of your dog.

Glossary

Altering: The neutering or spaying of an animal.

Booster jab: A vaccination that renews the effect of a previous one.

Breed: A group of animals within the same species, whose characteristics are passed down from generation to generation. Also means to mate and have offspring, or to organise breeding.

Breeder: A person or organisation that breeds a particular type of animal.

Carnivore: A meat-eating animal.

Domestication: The taming of animals by humans to keep them as pets or farm animals.

Distress: Pain, disturbance or discomfort usually caused by bad care.

Endangered species: A species whose numbers are becoming so low it is threatened with extinction.

Feral: A domestic animal that has become wild.

Hierarchy: A system of rank ordered according to status and authority.

Instinct: A natural, in-born feeling or reaction to something.

Litter: A family of puppies, all born from one pregnancy.

Mixed-breed (also called a mongrel): A dog whose parents are from two or more different breeds.

Neuter or spay: To operate on an animal so it can't have babies.

Parasites: Small animals that feed off another animal (a host). Also see entry for worms below.

Species: A group of animals that have characteristics in common, distinct from other animals, and that can reproduce together.

Vaccination: A medical treatment to prevent a particular disease, often given in the form of an injection. Also called a jab.

Worms: (in dogs, usually roundworms and tapeworms) Parasites that live inside an animal's digestive system and feed off its contents.

Websites

If you want to learn more about dogs, take lessons in dog training, or become involved in animal welfare, there are several helpful organisations you can contact. Your local pet centre can provide information about groups in your area. Try the Internet, too – some useful websites are listed here.

www.the-kennel-club.org.uk
The Kennel Club sets specifications for breeds and provides information on how to be a responsible dog owner. It has a list of reputable breeders and runs training classes, shows and exhibitions. There is a Young Kennel Club for 6–24-year-old dog lovers.

www.ankc.aust.com
The Australian National Kennel Club also sets breed standards and runs training courses and show trials. It promotes responsible ownership and can provide information on reliable breeders.

www.dogstrust.org.uk
The Dogs Trust (formerly NCDL, the National Canine Defence League) operates 15 rescue and re-homing centres throughout the UK. It has leaflets on choosing a dog and pet care, and produces teaching resources related to dog ownership. The website includes games and activities.

More general information on the care, health and welfare of pets is available from a number of organisations. These include:

www.rspca.co.uk
The RSPCA website has links to RSPCA websites throughout the world. It is full of information about animal adoption, news, care, training and education.

www.bluecross.org.uk
The Blue Cross – a charity for 'companion' animals, promoting pet care and responsibility towards animals in the community.

www.petplanet.co.uk
Facts and figures, news, activities and detailed breed profiles.

www.petwebsite.com
Information and articles on a wide range of pets and petcare options.

www.pethealthcare.co.uk
Advice on daily care, health problems, veterinary services and insurance.

Every effort has been made by the Publishers to ensure that these websites contain no inappropriate or offensive material. However, because of the nature of the Internet, it is impossible to guarantee that the contents of these sites will not be altered. We strongly advise that Internet access is supervised by a responsible adult.